IMAGES
of America

PLYMOUTH
CONNECTICUT

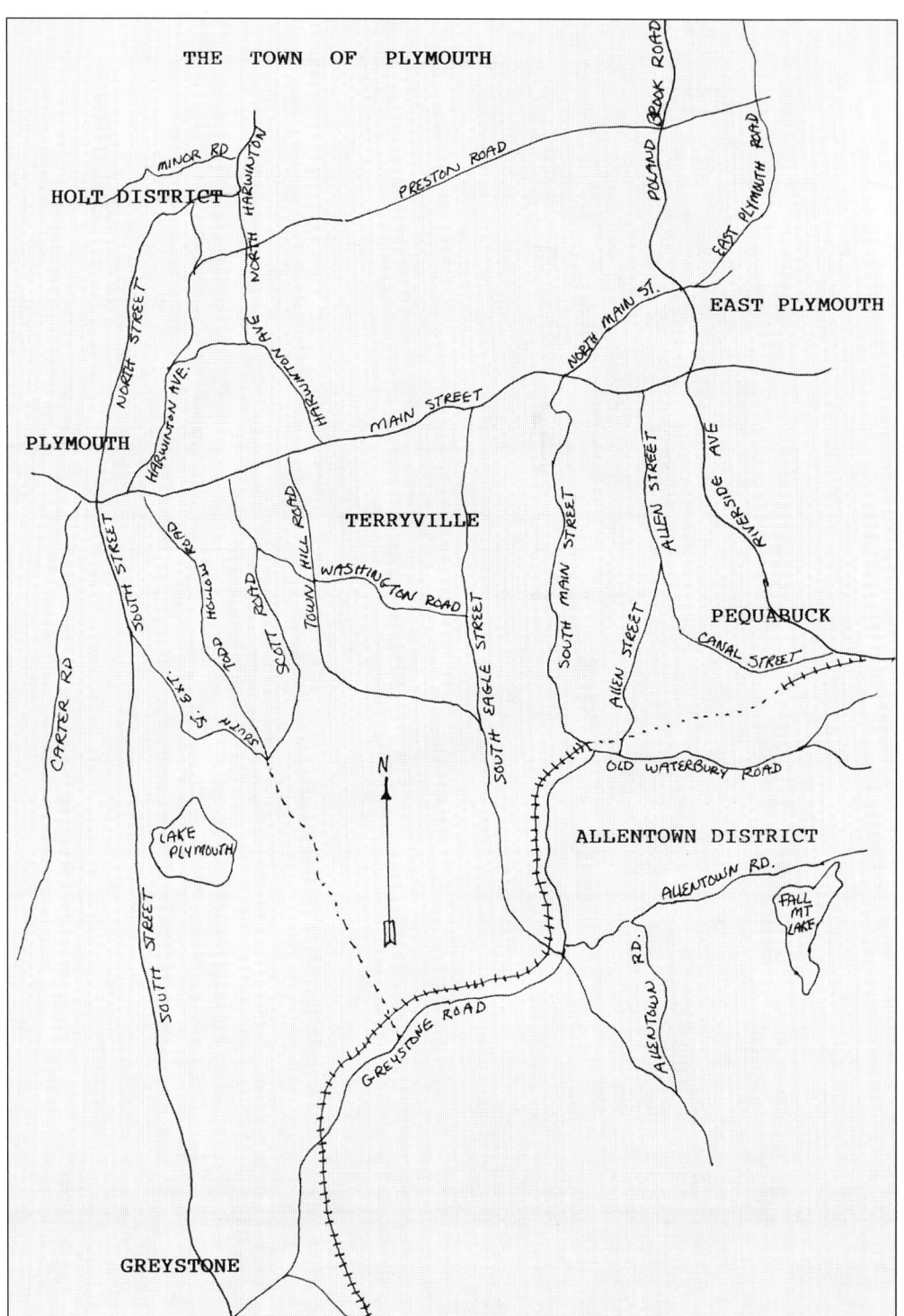

A map of the Town of Plymouth shows the many districts in the town and the placement of the villages of Plymouth, Terryville, and Pequabuck. The contents of the book will follow a counter-clockwise route beginning in Plymouth and ending in the Holt District.

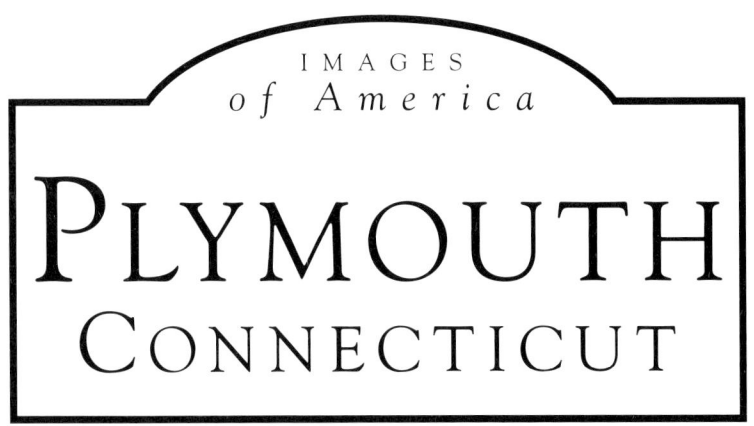

IMAGES of America
PLYMOUTH CONNECTICUT

Lani B. Johnson

First published 1996
Copyright © Lani B. Johnson, 1996

ISBN 0-7524-0500-4

Published by Arcadia Publishing,
an imprint of the Chalford Publishing Corporation
One Washington Center, Dover, New Hampshire 03820
Printed in Great Britain

Library of Congress Cataloging-in-Publication Data applied for

Contents

Acknowledgments 6

Introduction 7

1. Plymouth 9
2. Greystone, Tolles Station, and Allentown 31
3. Pequabuck 43
4. East Plymouth 49
5. Terryville 57
6. The Eagle Lock Company 89
7. Terryville Churches of the Past 97
8. The Holt District 105
9. People Who Serve 117

Acknowledgments

Plymouth has been my home since 1969, and I have grown to love this community and become part of its fiber. Writing this book has truly been a labor of love since it has brought me into the homes of so many people who graciously loaned irreplaceable pictures that captured precious memories from their past. Some pictures were removed from scrapbooks and taken down from living room walls and entrusted to me. I wish to thank the following people who provided information or rare and treasured photographs and postcards for use in this book: Joan Armbruster, April Beals, Theresa Blekis, Constance Blum, Chris Capolupo, Sandra Colasanto, Judy Miller Cumisky, Jack Duff of the Terryville Fire Department, Olive Ferry, Robert Henderson, Richard Johnson, Steve Kozikowski, Joe Lyga, Ferguson Mills of the O-Z/Gedney Company, Carol Minor Orr, Wesley and Ann Petrin, Barbara Pilbin, Myron Roman of the Thomaston Historical Society, Plymouth Town Clerk Janet Scoville, Elmon Smith, Robert and Kay Tolles, Russell and Alice Tolles, and Fred and Helen Wisneski.

The Plymouth Historical Society has provided me with an enormous amount of support and material for this book, and it is for the Plymouth Historical Society that I am writing this history. The special format of Arcadia's Images of America book series makes it possible to capture visually the history of the villages of Plymouth, Terryville, and Pequabuck that make up the Town of Plymouth.

I wish to credit two valuable sources that have been a tremendous help in researching this book: *The History of the Town of Plymouth Connecticut*, complied by Francis Atwater in 1895 and *Plymouth Connecticut: 1776–1976*, compiled by J. Francis Ryan.

I give very special thanks to Matt Malley, president of the Plymouth Historical Society, who is a true lover of history, a veritable encyclopedia of Plymouth's past, and who was an enormous source of encouragement and assistance with this publication. I also wish to thank Phyllis Corsetti for babysitting service. Lastly, I wish to acknowledge my husband, Leonard Johnson, for his patience and understanding.

Introduction

Nestled in the hills of southeastern Litchfield County, the Town of Plymouth boasts a proud colonial history beginning in the mid-seventeenth century. Almost 350 years ago, a hunting party ventured into the wilderness of what is now Plymouth and discovered a black lead mine. Anxious to take advantage of a potentially prosperous adventure, the party applied to the Tunxis Indian tribe, who controlled the area, for the right to work the mine. When the mine did not prosper, it was abandoned, and the Plymouth area did not become fully settled until some years later.

In the early part of the eighteenth century the area was wild and filled with deer, bear, and wolves. Hostile Indians from the north still traveled regularly through the area, and there was not a single cleared field. In 1710, a man named Holt was killed by Indians in the southern area of what is now Plymouth. Just five years before the first settler, Henry Cook, built his cabin in 1728, Indians killed and scalped a man working in the woods.

The Town of Plymouth was originally called Northbury. Many other European settlers followed Henry Cook into the village and petitioned for winter privileges in this new community. The name of Northbury was changed to Plymouth in 1795 when the town was officially incorporated. The hilly area around Town Hill Road where the annual Lions Club Terryville Country Fair is held was originally planned to be the center of this new town. Homes and businesses were built around the Town Hill area with a blacksmith shop on the corner of South Eagle Street and Washington Road. However, as time went by, the true center of town grew up around the Plymouth Green area on Main Street when the first town building was built there along with the two earliest churches in town. Businesses flourished and moved west toward Thomaston (then called Plymouth Hollow) and further east toward Terryville to take advantage of the natural water power found there.

In 1793, Eli Terry created a clock business that would become the foremost industry in the history of Plymouth. By 1809, Terry was working with Seth Thomas and Silas Hoadley in Greystone, but he sold his interest in the business to Thomas and Hoadley a year later. Together with his sons Henry and Eli Jr., Eli Terry introduced the well-known shelf clock and developed an enormously successful manufacturing business. The business eventually moved from Terry's bridge in Plymouth Hollow to a factory on the Pequabuck River in 1824. In 1833, Seth Thomas began the Seth Thomas Clock Company in Plymouth Hollow; the company later moved to Main Street in Thomaston. The village of Terryville was named for the Terry family, in particular Eli Terry Jr., who founded the village and built many homes for his workers in the farming community. Another son of Eli Terry, Silas Burnham Terry, established a second clock factory at the junction of Pequabuck and Poland Brooks. Eli Terry Jr.'s second son, Andrew

Terry, erected a building for the manufacture of malleable iron castings in Pequabuck. The O-Z/Gedney Company is now located on that spot.

In 1854, the Lewis Lock and James Terry Lock Companies merged to form the Eagle Lock Company, which became the most prosperous business in town. Terryville was chosen as the Town of Plymouth's business center because of the success and expansion of the Eagle Lock Company. Over the course of the nineteenth century, various small industries also developed along the many waterways in town. Companies that manufactured harness trimmings, wool, chairs, shears, plows, carriages, toys, blinds, hats, and wood products flourished in the Town of Plymouth.

A Town of Many Small Communities in a Circular Route around the Town of Plymouth.

Plymouth: In 1875, Plymouth Hollow officially became Thomaston by an act of the Connecticut State Legislature, and Thomaston became a separate community apart from Plymouth. Before the separation of Plymouth and Thomaston, there were fourteen schools in the community. All were one-room schoolhouses, and parents paid the school expenses. Each family was also required to provide wood for heating plus room and board for a specified number of days for the teacher.

In addition to the post office established in the village of Plymouth in 1812, additional post offices were established in Terryville and Pequabuck, the industrial areas of Plymouth. Before Thomaston split from Plymouth, another post office served the area of Plymouth Hollow beginning in 1837.

Greystone: Greystone developed as a community surrounding the clock factory owned by Eli Terry, Silas Hoadley, and Seth Thomas. This area was first known as Ireland, later as Hoadleyville, and finally as Greystone, now home to the Iseli Swiss Screw Machine Company and the Hancock Brook Dam.

Allentown District: This area south of Terryville was known as Indian Heaven. Many early residents are interred in the Allentown Cemetery on Allentown Road. The old Indian Heaven Rod and Gun Club began as a one-room schoolhouse in this district.

The Lakes: Both Lake Plymouth on South Street and Fall Mountain Lake began as recreational and farming areas and grew up as residential communities as the town gained in size and population.

Pequabuck: The town's railroads were located in the industrial community of Pequabuck to serve the Andrew Terry Company, the C.I. Allen wood turning company, the W.H. Scott and Company Store, and the Cooper Thermometer Company.

Terryville: Terryville became the business core of Plymouth after industry and population grew in this village center. The Terryville Post Office was established in 1831, and post office records show that the community's name was changed to Terryville somewhere around 1872.

East Plymouth: Also referred to as East Church, this historic area dates back to the Revolutionary War period. Several structures and areas still extant in East Plymouth date back to the 1750s, such as Tories Cave, Saint Matthew's Church and cemetery, and various homes.

The Holt District: In north Plymouth, the Holt District includes the Minor Estate and the Armbruster Farm, which was once owned by the Milo Holt family. Minor's property once extended westward to Lead Mine Brook. Lumber businesses and stone quarries were part of the history of Holt District, along with three taverns and the last one-room schoolhouse in the state. According to early records, Tories were hanged from a hook in one of the Holt District's taverns.

One
Plymouth

On the site of the present Plymouth Green, this early sketch shows the Old Training Ground prior to 1835. The Congregational church on the left was built in 1768 and was the second church to stand on this site. Saint Peter's Episcopal Church was built in 1796 and is located on the right of the picture behind the flagpole.

Eli Terry came to Plymouth in 1793 at the age of twenty-one and started to build his widely acclaimed wooden and brass clocks on Niagra Brook in Plymouth Hill, which was then called Northbury. After having ten children, Eli's wife Eunice died, and Eli married again and fathered two more children. He later moved his business from Hoadleyville (named for his partner Silas Hoadley) east to Terryville, where he built two houses. He is known for the thirty-hour clock, tower clocks, fine-quality cast brass clocks, and sheet metal clocks. Eli Terry died in 1852, and his sons continued in the business.

In 1746, the first meetinghouse in Plymouth was built. The second meetinghouse was completed in 1768.

The present Plymouth Congregational Church was built on Plymouth Green in 1838 and is home to the only wooden-works Eli Terry tower clock in the world. In 1853, a seminary for young ladies was established under the supervision of the church. Tuition was $120 a year. Part of the Hart Female Seminary became the Congregational parsonage when the school closed in 1857. A section of it now houses the Good News Thrift Shop, operated by the church.

Behind the Plymouth Congregational Church lies the old cemetery, where many early residents were laid to rest in the company of forty-two Revolutionary War soldiers, three veterans of the French and Indian War, and two veterans of the War of 1812.

An early sketch shows the east view of Plymouth as it began to grow in size. More buildings begin to appear next to the center of Plymouth and the church green.

The old Plymouth School, located on the northwest corner of Plymouth Green, was the first school built in Plymouth after the separation from Plymouth Hollow, now called Thomaston. The school was demolished when a new school was built on North Street in Plymouth. The winter term was taught by men, and the summer term was taught by women. The usual salary for a male teacher was $12 a month; female teachers made less than $1 a week.

Plymouth schoolchildren in 1894 stand for their picture to be taken. Teachers generally boarded with various parents of the children.

North Street in Plymouth was a dusty, unpaved road when it ran past the Plymouth School toward Plymouth Center.

Old Home Day in 1910 was a day for dressing up and celebrating on the Plymouth Green. Arthur Gordon took this early picture.

The old fire station in Plymouth was once located in the first town building and town hall. After the fire department moved out, the brick building was used by the Plymouth Historical Society and became its first museum.

An early postcard shows the business center of Plymouth. Facing east, one can see the stores, grange, and post office that once occupied the area around Plymouth Green. The old library that eventually burned down is the furthest building up on the left.

This home in Plymouth later became the Pierpont home and Episcopal rectory. George Pierpont was the town clerk of Plymouth and a member of the state legislature in the mid-nineteenth century. The building is also reputed to have been a tavern called the Red Tavern in earlier times.

The interior of Gates' store in Plymouth was neatly arranged with buggy whips, bolts of cloth, and basic supplies. Pauline Gates appears in the rear of the store.

Ralph Francis Gates, aged two years, is wearing a dress, as was quite common for little boys of this period. Not until a little boy was ready to start school did he give up his "dresses" for formal pictures.

A Plymouth Center postcard shows the old post office, which was established in 1812, and the library that burned in the early 1930s. Fannie Minor worked in the post office before her marriage to Maurice Minor. Now a half century later, Fannie's granddaughter, Betsy Minor Goodwin, works with the same postal service.

An early-nineteenth-century Fourth of July parade heads west in Plymouth. A Dairy Mart convenience store and gas station owned by Al and Kathleen Perkins now occupies the lot where the large, white Bradley's Candy Store in the center of the picture once stood. On the opposite corner is Beach and Blackmer's Store, now an apartment house.

Parades were always popular in small towns in New England. Costumed children are shown here marching up Main Street in Plymouth while celebrating the Fourth of July.

The Leach family from Plymouth poses for a full family formal portrait at the turn of the century. Only the little boy in the front seems to be enjoying the moment.

This older postcard shows Mattoon's Store and residence in Plymouth. The Mattoons sold the property to the Bradleys.

Bradley's Candy Store in Plymouth was located on the corner of South and East Main Streets.

Advertisements from the *Plymouth School News* in 1895 show that local businesses took advantage of the exposure the newspaper afforded as well as the railroad, which posted its schedule in the paper. The monthly publication cost 25¢ for a ten-month subscription.

TIME TABLE
N. Y., N. H. & H. R. R.

NAUGATUCK DIVISION.

Leave Thomaston for Waterbury, 7.43 and 10.23 A. M.; 2.55 and 5.26 P. M. SUNDAY, 3.47 P. M.

For Winsted 8.59 and 11.38 A. M.; 4.17 and 7.25 P. M. SUNDAY, 9.47 P. M.

Thomaston, Plymouth and Terryville stages meet every train at Thomaston and Terryville stations.

W. N. AUSTIN,
Hack, Livery,
—AND—
Feed Stables,

THOMASTON AND PLYMOUTH HILL.

Fine Carriages and Equipments, with careful attendants, always in readiness.

Piano and Furniture Moving a Specialty

Express Orders Attended to Promptly.

There is nothing preserves and improves your Carriage or Sleigh like a good job of Painting, and the Best place for quality of work and material is at . . .

FRANK L. BUNNELL'S
BLAKESLEE'S SHOP.
PLYMOUTH, CONN.

PRICES RIGHT.
Also New and Second Hand Carriages for Sale or Exchange.

From a snowy field, an early photographer caught the growing Town of Plymouth from a distance.

Facing east toward the center of Plymouth, the newly plowed road is lined with large trees.

The Saint Peter's Episcopal parish was first organized in 1740, but didn't hold its first service until 1796, when the congregation moved from Thomaston. The original Saint Peter's Episcopal Church was built on the northeast corner of Plymouth Green.

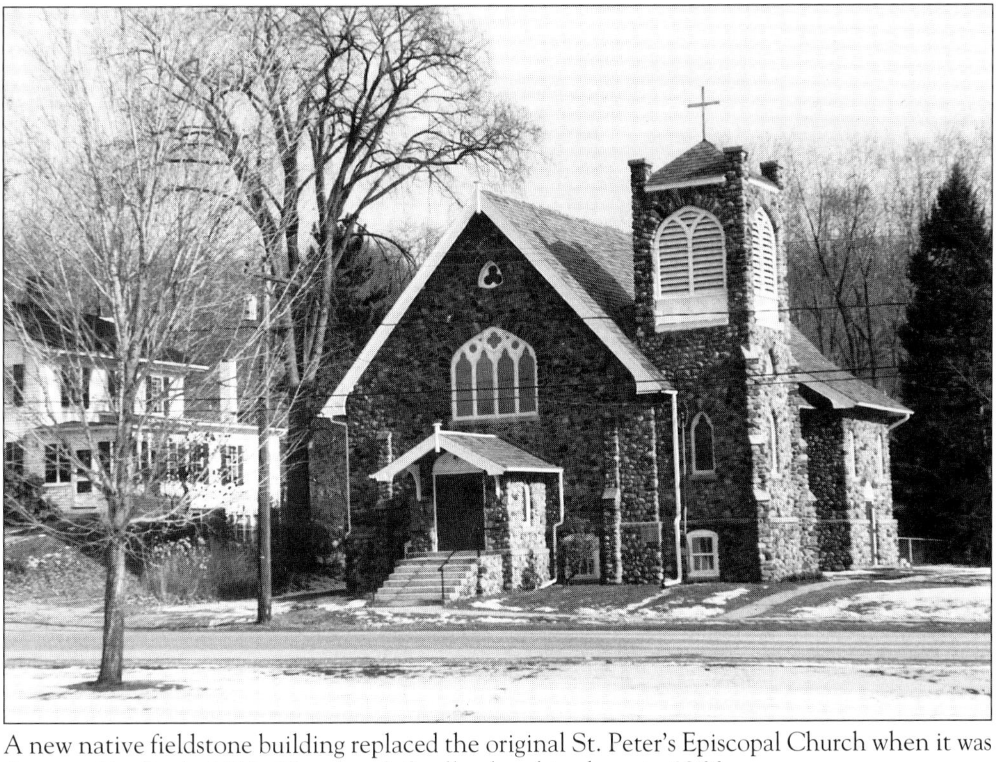

A new native fieldstone building replaced the original St. Peter's Episcopal Church when it was destroyed by fire in 1915. The church finally closed its doors in 1966.

Bryon Tuttle was born in Plymouth in 1825 and established a carriage business with A.C. Shelton. His home, located in Plymouth, now belongs to the Cleaveland family next to the Country Store. Members of the Tuttle family were charter members of the Turnpike Corporation.

Cleaveland's Country Store has been a continual source of ice cream, candy, music boxes, and antiques for many years. One attraction has been the carved cigar-store Indian that guarded the entrance. The Indian was stolen at one time but was later found in a Yale dormitory and returned to his rightful place.

Edward Botelle supplied this 1909 picture of "Gramp" Botelle with his wagon and the whips that he sold throughout Plymouth and nearby towns.

Young ladies, in white dresses and ribbons, surround Lady Liberty in this early Fourth of July

celebration in front of the Plymouth Congregational Church.

The Plymouth Grange No. 72 was organized in 1887 as a subordinate organization to the Great Order of Patrons of Husbandry. The grange held meetings and fairs that dealt with all issues pertaining to the home or farm. The building still stands and is now used by Tim's Antiques as a warehouse.

This early home was built in high Victorian style by George Langdon. The home, somewhat changed, is still located next to the Plymouth Library.

Lake Plymouth was formed in the early 1800s when "Uncle Vic" Tomlison cleared the land and flooded about 45 acres, creating "Uncle Vic's Pond."

The center of Plymouth was once a dirt road that left the intersection of North, South, and Main Streets a grassy patch to be skirted around with horse and buggy.

A re-enactment of Revolutionary War days was performed in front of a house on South Street in 1952. College students and local Plymouth residents are shown here acting out the farewells given two hundred years before to men going off to fight in the Revolution.

Two
Greystone, Tolles Station, and Allentown

In 1809, Eli Terry joined with fellow clock makers Seth Thomas and Silas Hoadley to construct a clock factory near the Greystone Falls. After Terry and Thomas left to build other factories, Silas Hoadley built the Hoadley Clock Factory, which was to continue throughout the century in the area of Greystone called Hoadleyville. The falls below the factory—located on the right of the picture—provided the power needed to run the factory and gristmill.

In the center of the picture, below the Hoadley factory (where the property bordered Waterville), the remains of a gristmill once owned by Calvin Hoadley can be seen. The mill used a water wheel for power as did most mills at that time.

This late 1800s picture shows the Hoadley factory on the left and a home on the right that once belonged to a lawyer named Bronson. The house was torn down, and today parts of the old foundation are still visible behind the houses of Olive Ferry and Mr. and Mrs. Ward Ferry Jr. The home of Viola Peterson sits on the original site of the Hoadley factory; Viola's father-in-law once worked in the factory, which went bankrupt in 1907.

The Greystone School was a one-room schoolhouse located near the Hoadley factory. Many of the original families in this area were Irish, a fact which led to the community's originally being named "Ireland." Pictured here in front of the school are children from the Peterson, Dingwell, Lombaro, Johnson, Block, Bodian, Marterli, and Russell families. Teachers Ruby North and Carrie Johnson once lived upstairs in the Johnson farmhouse, now the home of Thomas and Sandra Colasanto.

The Greystone railroad station was located near the Hoadley factory. The small station was well maintained and had a raised platform to facilitate loading freight. The Hancock station near Al Cibelli's horse farm was located 2 miles down the tracks, and a mile further down was the Tolles station at the foot of Lane Hill Road.

A passenger train roars up the tracks along South Main Street in its approach to Tolles station.

The Tolles railroad station was located near the tracks on South Main Street and Lane Hill. Passengers waiting for the train would raise a flag to signal it to stop. Joe Lyga remembered that in the 1920s, an old hermit lived near the station in a shack. While walking the tracks from Terryville to Waterbury, the hermit once spotted a large boulder on the rails and alerted the on-coming train. The railroad rewarded the man by providing him daily with food and a newspaper.

The Greystone area had a reputation for housing large rattlesnakes in its rocks and ledges. The original caption attached to this picture of young boys in early Greystone is recorded as "rattlesnake hunters."

Albert Johnson stands proudly next to his bicycle in 1918.

The Johnson Farm on Greystone Road was purchased between 1910 and 1917 by four Johnson brothers: Theodore, Herbert, Arthur, and Carl. They bought the farm from D.B. Wilson, who had raised Dutch-belted cattle there for many years. When the Hancock Dam was built north of the farm after the 1955 flood, much of this land was taken for the dam. This 1949 photograph shows the barns and the farmhouse.

The red brick farmhouse, built in the late eighteenth century, still sits near the Hancock Dam and is owned by Sandra Johnson Colasanto and her husband Thomas. There was once a brickyard on the property that supplied the bricks for this fine old house.

This group is ready for winter fun on their sleds in front of the old Johnson Farm milk house. From left to right are Sandra, Lois, and Walter Johnson, young Bunny Bright, and her mom, Celia Bright.

Dairy cattle were once raised on over 1,000 acres of the Johnson Farm; later, the Johnsons decided to raise turkeys instead. In the background of this rare picture, one can see the turkeys covering the old Greystone Road in front of the farmhouse.

Several Tolles family farms once occupied much of the area surrounding South Main Street and Lane Hill Road. In this early picture of the old Tolles barn and hay fields, oxen pull in wagons loaded with hay. Ancestors of the Tolles family immigrated from England in 1632 and settled in Plymouth in the late 1700s. Bob Tolles, his sister, and cousin Russell Tolles (son of Irving Tolles) are ninth-generation Americans, proud of their long history in Connecticut.

The Tolles family and their in-laws, the Thomas family, pose on the Fourth of July in the early 1920s. Included in the picture are Robert Tolles and his cousin, Russell Fenn Tolles, as sailor-suited "cherubs." Carrie Tolles, Bob's mother, stands on the left; grandma Fidelia Tolles stands behind the seated Aunt Hattie Oddy.

Walter and Fidelia Bassett Tolles with Aunt Hattie Oddy feed the chickens in this early-twentieth-century photograph. The Tolles barn can still be seen across from the original Lane Hill Road farmhouse, which Robert and Kay Tolles have lovingly maintained in its original state (with some remodeling). The farmhouse contains much of the original 24-foot-wide wood paneling inside.

The one-room schoolhouse in Allentown District was later bought by the Indian Heaven Rod and Gun Club. The small building was then enlarged into a large clubhouse. Many people in town will remember attending parties and breakfasts at Indian Heaven until it burned down and the land was sold for a home.

Walter Tolles is shown picking up a large sheaf of grain in order to thresh it in the barn on the Tolles Farm on Lane Hill Road. The tool he is using is called a flail. Walter's ancestor, Lamberton Tolles Sr., came to settle in Plymouth in 1798 and began farming.

Two hikers pose by Jack's Cave, located in a once remote series of ledges near the man-made Fall Mountain Lake. The cave was named after "Indian Jack," who made his home there.

Buttermilk Falls was affiliated with both the Tolles Farm and the nearby Bassett Farm for two hundred years. At the top of the falls, the Tolles once operated a sawmill; the dam and hole for the large overshot wheel can still be seen. This early postcard shows Bristol resident Silas Carrington sitting by the falls.

Located off the narrow, winding, one-rod-wide (about 17 feet) Lane Hill Road, Buttermilk Falls is now part of the Nature Conservancy. The remarkable hidden falls are a protected preserve and are part of the Blue Trail. In 1977, a local committee worked to raise funds to purchase the 13-acre parcel and keep the falls as an undisturbed natural resource for the town.

Three
Pequabuck

The Horseshoe Falls are a scenic wonder in Pequabuck. Once used to power the Terry foundry, they remain a delightful sight on Canal Street.

Eli Terry Jr.'s son Andrew, born in 1824, established a pioneer business in malleable iron casting in Terryville.

Founded by Andrew Terry in 1847, the O-Z/Gedney Company was originally called the Malleable Iron Works. In 1871, D. Hunter and R.D.H. Allen bought the company, and in 1896 it became the Andrew Terry Company. During World War II, a New York company merged with Andrew Terry to become the Gedney Electric Company. After Olsen and Zeller invented a cast-metal cable device for elevators, their manufacturing company was purchased by General Signal Corporation, who later also bought the Gedney Company. This merger created the O-Z/Gedney Company in 1974.

In 1896, Andrew Terry executives posed in the main office. Pictured are, from left to right: George Clark, Jonathon Stair, Mr. Bushnell, Edgar Pond, and Charles Livingston.

The Horseshoe Falls, located on Canal Street across from the water treatment plant, were constructed to provide water for the Andrew Terry Foundry, now the O-Z/Gedney Company. The bridge in the foreground crossed over the Pequabuck River. A new bridge named for successful actor and "hometown boy" Ted Knight was later built.

The railroad to Terryville was greatly enhanced by the construction of the Pequabuck Tunnel, which was completed in 1910. The one-mile tunnel was called the Sylvan Hill Tunnel, and many residents remember people being lost in the tunnel or children daring each other to walk through the scary dark tube. The last passenger train to be operated through Terryville ran in 1960.

An early postcard from Pequabuck celebrates the newly constructed railroad arch over the Pequabuck River.

New Railroad Station, Terryville, Conn.

The Pequabuck railroad station was located across the street from the W.H. Scott Store, a prominent business in Pequabuck that sold everything from grain, shoes, coal, and patent medicines to wood from their sawmill. Passengers from Terryville and Pequabuck used this station to catch trains.

These two daring young women pose in the early 1900s on a handcar on the railroad tracks near the Pequabuck railroad station as railroad workers do some repair work in the background.

The Pequabuck School was designated District No. 13 School and was erected on School Street in Pequabuck. The two-story school was later used for storage purposes by the Cooper Thermometer Company. Horace Whittier joined the Cooper company in 1912 and became president in the early 1930s. The company was sold in the 1950s.

A fire that burned the Terry foundry in 1894 curtailed its manufacturing activity for a while, but the company remained operating and has been doing so continuously for almost a hundred and fifty years.

Four
East Plymouth

Saint Matthew's Church was built by Tories who were loyal members of the Church of England. People lived around the church in farms scattered along the hillsides.

The house on top of the hill was built around 1830 by Wylls Hinman. It was later owned by the Franklin Tolles family, and is now owned by Paul and April Beals. Franklin Tolles was a peddler and had a store in his home at one time. The original lower house burned, and a new home, now the home of John Laser, was erected on the spot in the late nineteenth century. The small barn in front once housed a store and later a machine shop.

In the center of East Plymouth, also called East Church, stood the Orrin Preston house (on the left), which was built around 1860. A general store operated out of the house and also out of a back room in the old Scoville house that stands next door. The store was known as "Schwabies Store" at one time.

A snowy road leads into East Plymouth. Many small businesses and industries thrived in the area surrounding Saint Matthew's Church, including a tannery, a blacksmith, a toy factory, a nail-making shop, a carding mill, and Eli Terry's original sawmill.

The road from East Plymouth to Terryville led south down a country lane past farms and small businesses.

Iona Ely Smith and her daughter Helena sit in front of the old Scoville house while Helena's husband, Thomas Scoville, stands nearby. Leon and Beatrice Scoville lived in the house before the property was purchased by Chris and John Capolupo.

East Plymouth resident John Tolles, son of Franklin Tolles, stands with Luella, his new bride, in this 1920 portrait. They lived in the Tolles house next to the Old Marsh where John rented boats to visitors.

Members of the Tolles family cut wood near a shed on the property. The Old Marsh Pond can be seen in the background.

The Old Marsh Pond was used for grazing cattle, swimming, and fishing before it was purchased by the Bristol Water Company. A toy factory existed at the bottom of the hill across from the dam; its foundation still exists.

Saint Matthew's Church was founded in East Plymouth near Tories Den in 1792 by the Second Episcopal Society of Plymouth. Around 1842, the 42-by-32-foot church was turned around and placed where it now stands as a private home.

The East Plymouth cemetery next to Saint Matthew's Church was the final resting place for many of the early inhabitants of Plymouth. This picture taken in 1906 shows both the humped marker form developed from the traditional "death's-head-and-wings"-shape tombstone and the rectangular cemetery marker shape from the early 1800s. The only Tory to be hanged for treason, Moses Dunbar, is buried in this cemetery. Reports state that Dunbar's own father offered to provide the rope to hang him.

A wanderer known as the "Leather Man" existed in Plymouth in the nineteenth century. Dressed all in leather, he never spoke or smiled. He traveled a circular route each year from 1862 to 1889, beginning in Harwinton and going through East Plymouth, south to Saybrook, west to New York State, and north again to Harwinton and Plymouth. "The Leather Man" is assumed to have been the Frenchman Jules Bourglay, who became desperate after losing his job in the leather market and the girl he loved.

This rare photograph taken through the back door of a home in East Plymouth is one of the last pictures ever taken of the infamous "Leather Man." Much thinner and looking quite frail, he was to die soon after this. A mystery figure and lonely soul, the "Leather Man" died while traveling his compulsive circular route through Connecticut and New York.

In the northeast corner of Plymouth there is a popular trail that leads to the foot of a cliff called Tories Den. This natural cave is composed of rock formations, and it was used supposedly by Indians, the Tories, and the famed "Leather Man" in early times. Stephen Graves once hid in the cave to escape Tory-hunters; after its use in the Revolutionary War, both ends of the cave were closed up. In 1838, Tories Den was rediscovered by two fourteen-year-old boys.

Five
Terryville

Eli Terry Jr., the eldest son of Eli Terry, was the founder of the village of Terryville. He was active in the Congregational churches both in Plymouth and Terryville. He built many homes in Terryville and also built a water wheel to aid his business. Eli Jr. successfully manufactured clocks and locks until his death at the age of forty-two in 1841. This house on Main Street is identified as a Terry house and was located near Eli Terry's original business in Terryville.

The Judd Farm was located on North Main Street and has been identified as one of the oldest homes in Terryville.

Wilbert N. Austin owned the Thomaston and Plymouth stage line as well as a livery stable once located behind the Austin House. His business was responsible for carrying the mail between post offices and railroads. This old poster advertises such an early stage.

The Red Bridge was once located at the intersection of the present Routes 6 and 72 and functioned as the main entrance into Terryville village from the east. When the trolley came into Terryville, the tracks came across the Red Bridge to and from Bristol.

A 1912 postcard shows a bird's-eye view of Terryville.

A high camera angle captures an early picturesque view of Terryville.

The Immaculate Conception Church is seen here from across the park on the corner of Park Street and Main. The old Lyceum is to the right. The Terryville Furniture store later took over the Lyceum building, added to it, and conducted a prosperous business for many years.

Baldwin Park once sported a pond in the green, but this was drained years ago. The Terryville Institute is still standing to the right in this picture at the other end of the park.

In 1902, the first trolley car entered Terryville. The Bristol Tramway Company extended their line to make travel between Terryville and Bristol easier. The trolley line went through Pequabuck and ran up Main Street to Harwinton Avenue.

The trolley tracks were constructed to meet the railroad crossing at Pequabuck and continued on the other side of the railroad tracks, where another trolley would finish the Terryville journey. When the road was later lowered, it was possible for the trolley to make the entire run without changing trolley cars. In this picture, the trolley tracks enter Terryville across the bridge at Riverside and Route 6. Trolley cars were abandoned as a mode of travel in the early 1930s.

Motorman John H. Thomas (on the left) brought the first trolley to Terryville. In 1925, the date of this picture, former Terryville resident Raymond Strupp (on the right) was the conductor for the run that originally stopped at W.H. Scott's Store in Pequabuck.

Trolley tracks move up Main Street past the Terryville Institute. The school and tracks no longer exist, but the building on the corner of North Main Street still stands as an apartment house.

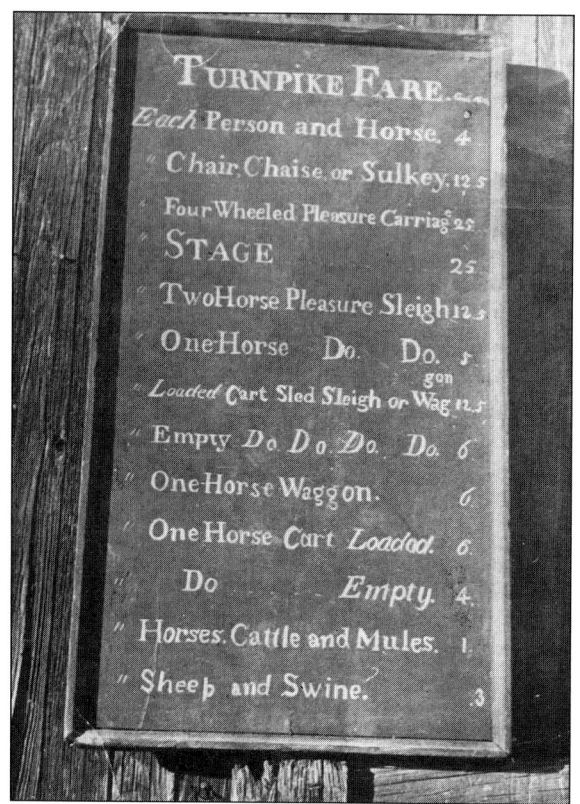

From 1834 to 1860, Route 6 was a toll road that traveled up to Litchfield. The tollhouse was located next to the Alley house (now the home of the Plymouth Historical Society), and a gate keeper and toll collector stayed in the small building west of the house. A reproduction of the toll rate sign is posted on the building.

The Terryville Institute began as a school on Main Street (where the veteran's memorial now stands) housing grades one through twelve. The institute was used as a school until the present Terryville High School was built; the building was then demolished.

A group of female students pose with their teacher. Included in the picture are Ada Pratt, Arlene Austin, and Katherine Whitney.

65

The Terryville Town Hall was situated on the site of the present lock museum on the corner of Prospect and Main Streets. It was here that this author's lawyer completed a title search by looking through records kept in old shoe boxes in the basement. Times have changed.

The town hall got a facelift and had an addition added to the front in 1911, which provided more space for the growing town.

The Plymouth Town Farm was originally acquired in 1913 and was maintained as an efficient dairy farm until the 1970s. The main section of the old farmhouse was used by the caretaker and his family, while the rear building housed the "inmates," as they were called in earlier times. Vagrants, alcoholics, and homeless men lived at the farm and worked for their keep. Some men came on their own; others were assigned here.

Bernice Blekis stands in front of the town farmhouse, located on North Harwinton Avenue, in the mid-1950s. Bernice and her husband Peter bought the town farm after World War II and continued to run it as a home for working residents until Bernice died in 1977. Grandchildren Theresa, Paul, and Tony Blekis remember spending part of their childhood here.

This postcard view of Main Street looking east in Terryville shows the corner of South Main Street, where Terryville Pizza and Terryville True Value Hardware now conduct business. The building pictured here contains the old Terryville Post Office, the A&P grocery store, and the Terryville Hardware Store. Theodore Piotrowski bought the whole block on South Main from Amos Lister and ran the two-story Terryville Hardware Store from his return home after World War II until the 1970s.

Trolley tracks once came up Main Street in Terryville past the Austin House on the left and the hardware store and post office on the right.

The Shear Shop was located on Main Street near the intersection of Riverside Avenue. It was later converted into a tenement building that stood where the Eagles Hall is now located.

Eugene Park was located off Ashton Drive in a secluded area complete with a pond and social hall that was used for wedding receptions and parties. According to William Allread, the present owner, the park was once owned by the New York Giants and later by the VFW. It was named for a local man who returned to Poland and was killed in the World War II. Today the pond still exists, but the building is no longer there.

Workers struggle to clear snow from Main Street after a storm in March of 1920. It looks like everyone pitched in with picks and shovels to help. The old hotel, which was razed after a fire, is on the right of the picture.

Older residents in town may remember the boarding house that was situated up from the Prospect Street School. Until the building was torn down in the early 1900s, many Eagle Lock workers and local teachers lived here. Vincent and Dorothy Malley remember that Patrick Salmon ran this boarding house and that his daughter Margaret later ran another boarding house next to the Terryville Congregational Church.

In 1930, Prospect Street sported telephone poles and a sidewalk, but it was still an often-muddy, unpaved road.

One-room district schools were popular with parents who were anxious to keep their children in their own neighborhood. However, growing school populations accompanied the growth of Terryville industry, and larger, consolidated schools became necessary. The large, brick Prospect Street School was built in the early 1900s to keep pace with the times.

This picture—taken in 1912—shows a temporary facility that was nicknamed the "Prospect Street School Chicken Coop" by people who felt some contempt for this early means of creating interim classroom space. Mrs. Harry S. Fisher taught here at one time.

Scrubbed and picture-pretty with bows and crossed legs, these elementary school students posed on the steps of the Prospect Street School with their teacher in the early part of this century.

Older youngsters pose in front of the Prospect School, which also served as the high school before the present high school was built.

SWIMMING HOLE
MIDDLE POND
TERRYVILLE, CONN.

A local man sits near the old swimming hole at Middle Pond. Both Upper and Middle Ponds are now owned by the Terryville Fish and Game Club, but they were once owned by Eagle Lock and were used to provide water for the water-wheel power generating system.

Men and horses are shown here in an early photograph cutting ice from Middle Pond.

Zeiner-Seymour Pond, Terryville, Conn.

Lake Winfield off Seymour Road was once called Zeiner-Seymour Pond. About twenty years ago, the lake was drained and rebuilt by the U.S. Army Corps of Engineers. Lake Winfield is now a popular place for anglers, joggers, picnickers, and swimmers.

LAKEVIEW CABINS
ROUTE 6 AND ROUTE 202
TERRYVILLE, CONN.
TEL. 2-0400

Lakeview Cabins, providing vacation homes for weekend visitors, once lined the southern portion of Walter Zeiner's pond. There were cooking facilities, toilets, and hot-water faucets in each cabin.

Trolley tracks continued up toward Harwinton Avenue past the hardware store on the right.

This photograph of the "Great White Way" in Terryville shows the many small businesses that made up downtown Terryville. The Whole Donut is now located in this area.

The famous Terryville cannon—located near Baldwin Park—is dedicated to Dorence Atwater, who enlisted in the Civil War at the age of eighteen and was later captured and sent to the horrible prison at Andersonville. Assigned to the surgeon's office, Atwater kept detailed records of the thirteen thousand deaths at the prison. After his release, he managed to smuggle the records back to Connecticut to determine the fate of missing men. Atwater later worked with Clara Barton to properly mark the graves of the dead.

This is the first lock museum in America, shown here on Main Street east of its present location in Terryville. The museum started its collection with a large donation from the Eagle Lock Company and continues to exhibit the largest collection of early American locks in the world.

Reinholdt Schwanka's sketch for the 1976 bicentennial calendar shows the water wheel on Main Street before the Plymouth Historical Society restored it to its original condition and enclosed it in a protective kiosk.

Downtown Terryville was the location of Carl Miller's popular luncheonette and fountain in the 1940s. The restaurant was located near where the Whole Donut Shop is today. Carl later owned a shoe store that many people in the Town of Plymouth will remember.

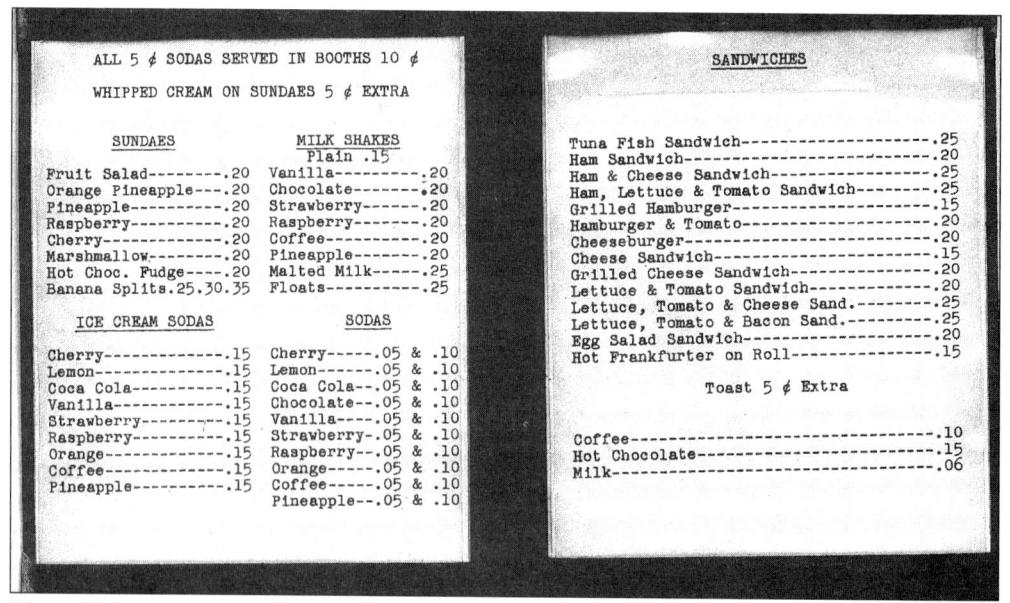

```
ALL 5¢ SODAS SERVED IN BOOTHS 10¢
WHIPPED CREAM ON SUNDAES 5¢ EXTRA

     SUNDAES              MILK SHAKES
                           Plain .15
Fruit Salad--------.20  Vanilla---------.20
Orange Pineapple----.20 Chocolate-------.20
Pineapple----------.20  Strawberry------.20
Raspberry----------.20  Raspberry-------.20
Cherry-------------.20  Coffee----------.20
Marshmallow--------.20  Pineapple-------.20
Hot Choc. Fudge----.20  Malted Milk-----.25
Banana Splits.25.30.35  Floats----------.25

  ICE CREAM SODAS           SODAS
Cherry-------------.15  Cherry------.05 & .10
Lemon--------------.15  Lemon-------.05 & .10
Coca Cola----------.15  Coca Cola---.05 & .10
Vanilla------------.15  Chocolate---.05 & .10
Strawberry---------.15  Vanilla-----.05 & .10
Raspberry----------.15  Strawberry--.05 & .10
Orange-------------.15  Raspberry---.05 & .10
Coffee-------------.15  Orange------.05 & .10
Pineapple----------.15  Coffee------.05 & .10
                        Pineapple---.05 & .10
```

```
                SANDWICHES

Tuna Fish Sandwich--------------------.25
Ham Sandwich-------------------------.20
Ham & Cheese Sandwich----------------.25
Ham, Lettuce & Tomato Sandwich--------.25
Grilled Hamburger--------------------.15
Hamburger & Tomato-------------------.20
Cheeseburger------------------------.20
Cheese Sandwich----------------------.15
Grilled Cheese Sandwich--------------.20
Lettuce & Tomato Sandwich------------.20
Lettuce, Tomato & Cheese Sand.-------.25
Lettuce, Tomato & Bacon Sand.--------.25
Egg Salad Sandwich-------------------.20
Hot Frankfurter on Roll--------------.15

              Toast 5¢ Extra

Coffee------------------------------.10
Hot Chocolate-----------------------.15
Milk--------------------------------.06
```

This old fountain menu from Miller's Luncheonette and Fountain shows prices that haven't been seen for a long time. A hamburger and a coke cost Miller's customers a mere 20¢, and another 25¢ bought them a banana split. Add another zero to approximate today's prices.

Near Miller's luncheonette was the old Mayfair Theater. A double feature, cartoons, a carnival glass dish, a cliff-hanger short, and previews might cost one 10¢.

Across the street from the Mayfair Theater was the Mayfair Garage, which still stands in the same location as the Mayfair Sunoco (now owned by Frank Fuller). Gas prices are not the same, however!

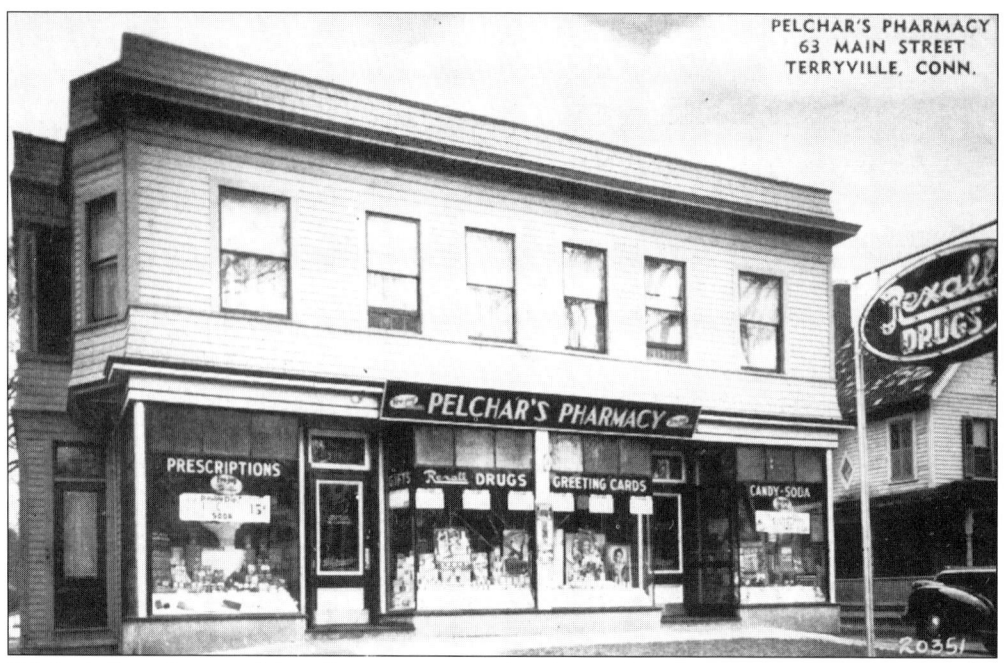

PELCHAR'S PHARMACY
63 MAIN STREET
TERRYVILLE, CONN.

Pelchar's Drug Store on Main Street was a popular place to buy ice cream cones, postcards, and prescriptions before the building became Silvio's Restaurant. Not too many years ago, Pelchar's sold double-dip ice cream cones for 15¢.

The Harry S. Fisher School, constructed in the 1950s, was named in honor of a popular one-time school superintendent. (As a footnote, the "S" stands for Sylvester.) The Fisher School's athletic field was named for Raymond T. Malley, who graduated from Terryville High School and later also became superintendent of the town's schools.

A FREE *Raybestos* SERVICE that will save you $$$
Next time you stop in, ask us to "PULL A WHEEL"

- You're just wasting money to get a brake adjustment when the linings are too worn. Furthermore, there's the danger of scoring the brake drums . . . and that costs a lot more than new Brake Linings.

- There is only one SURE way to prevent this needless expense and keep your brakes working at Maximum SAFETY . . . that is to "Pull a Wheel" and examine the actual condition of your brakes.

- Pulling a Wheel is part of our FREE Raybestos Brake Service.

MIDWAY GARAGE
W. Main Street   Phone 8719
Terryville, Conn.

There's NO OBLIGATION

A early postcard advertisement from Midway Garage on West Main Street in Terryville offered brake repair and free inspections.

An Esso gas station was located on Main Street near where Elm Street is now. Hagerman's gas station was located across the street from the present Shea Chevrolet business.

The High Farm Dairy on Town Hill Road was originally established by Joseph Kozikowski Sr. and his wife Helen in 1919. There were six boys and four girls to help with milking forty cows and taking in huge loads of hay. Only the barn on the right of this picture stands on the land now.

The High Farm Dairy delivered milk via horse and wagon before purchasing a fleet of trucks. Here, Irene Kozikowski and her sweetheart cuddle for the camera in front of a milk truck.

Youngsters frolic on a loaded hay truck on the High Farm on July 5, 1942. Steve Kozikowski remembers that when the hay was ready, all the neighbors pitched in to bring in the loose hay. In this way, local farmers all helped each other.

Upland Farm was established by Joseph and Joanna Pawelchak in 1915. The old farmhouse was torn down to allow the construction of the Knight Lane Estates off Scott Road. Joseph Pawelchak peddled milk by horse-drawn wagon until 1940, and until his death in 1972, he continued farming with his grandson, Wesley Petrin.

Joseph Pawelchak's son John remembers that during hard times in the Depression, his father might accept a shot of homemade moonshine in exchange for the family's milk at several homes on his milk route. Thankfully, the horse knew the way home.

Joanna Pawelchak and her husband immigrated from the same village in the Ukraine to Terryville as teenagers. Joanna always cooked on the huge cast-iron stove that dominated her kitchen. Neighbors on Scott Road will remember watching Joanna and her daughter Nellie walking the cows down the road to pasture until the early 1970s.

Edmund Borkoski is a regular figure at the Terryville Fair. Here he stands with his prized team of Brown Swiss oxen, named Tom and Jerry (in fact, all of his teams are named Tom and Jerry). For fifty years Ed has competed in oxen draws throughout New England.

The annual Terryville Fair is sponsored by the Terryville Lions Club. First organized in 1941, the fair has continued to be a successful major state event. A popular attraction is often the horse-pulling contest, which sometimes features a three-horse pulling team like the powerful group shown here.

The Townhill Schoolhouse was built in 1800 across from the entrance to the present Lions Club Terryville Fairgrounds. According to the memories of Galus Fenn, in 1858 the school was referred to as the "high school." At one time eighty children attended the one-room school—a large class for any teacher! In spite of struggling in its crowded quarters, many successful graduates went on to become attorneys, judges, and one even became a mayor of Stamford.

Officer Paul Beals directs traffic in front of the Austin House, which had suffered a fire. The Austin House was built in 1865 and was a regular stop for the stagecoach service. Under the management of Grant Austin and later Winfred Gleason, the Austin House became a residence and commissary for Eagle Lock workers. In the early 1950s, Fred and Helen Wisneski bought the landmark business and ran it until 1986. The Austin House remains a popular meeting place and bar.

Six
The Eagle Lock Company

In 1854, after a long history of problems, several lock companies consolidated as the Eagle Lock Company, with James Terry as president. The company would grow into a major manufacturing complex in the following years, eventually dominating the area bounded by South Main, Eagle, and South Eagle Streets.

Large teams of horses were used to load heavy materials to and from the Eagle Lock factory. Finished products were often brought to the Pequabuck railroad station in order to ship them to ready markets around the world. There used to be a drive-through scale on Agney Avenue that was used to weigh coal and other products.

This picture from the collection of the Minor family shows a rare interior view of the factory. This spotless workstation changed little over the years.

In 1908, the Eagle Lock Company provided work for hundreds of new immigrants to the Town of Plymouth and became the largest employer in town. The diverse traditions of the workers who moved to Terryville Village helped to create the many cultural and religious institutions in the town. This postcard shows the main office of Eagle Lock.

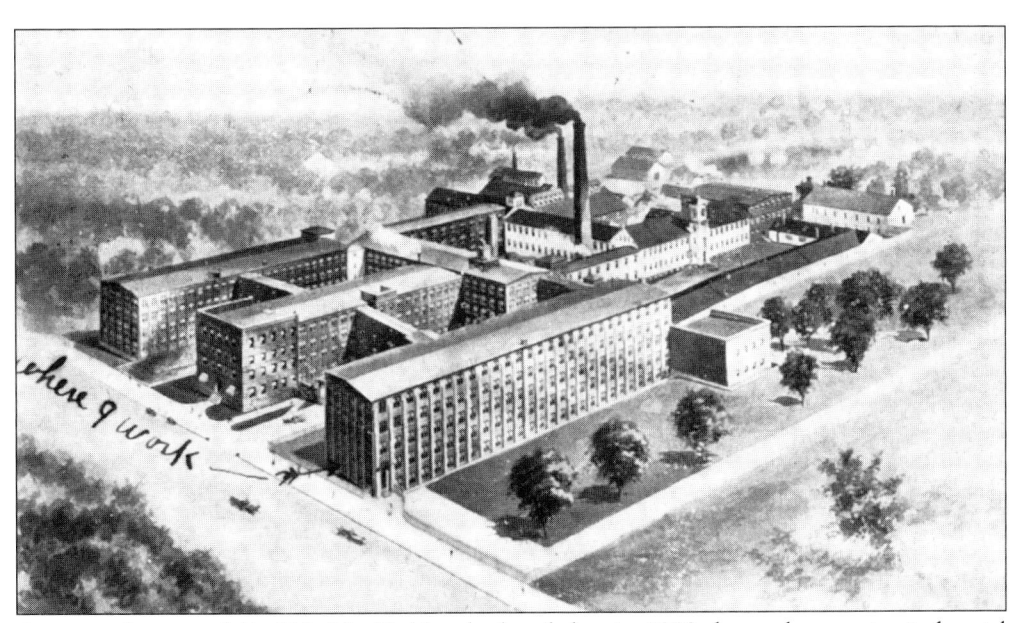

A postcard sent to Miss Ethel L. Holders by her father in 1910 shows the massive industrial complex that made up the Eagle Lock Company. Notice where Miss Holder's father has indicated that he worked.

Turn-of-the-century workers at Eagle Lock wore aprons for work. Notice the very young age of some of the workers, who had quit school in order to start their working lives in the factory.

Child-labor laws have changed drastically in the last one hundred years.

This picture shows the long-gone Eagle Lock shop, which was located across from the present-day Western Auto Store on Main Street. The water wheel that provided power to run the shop has been restored to its original location.

This rare old photograph features Eagle Lock pin room employees in 1904. Women had entered the work force some time earlier, and many joined the ranks at the factory.

This facing view of the Eagle Lock Company shows the present-day location of the Napco Plant #3 on South Main Street. At one time, Eagle Lock made a complete line of wood screws, mousetraps, bottle openers, and soap-box derby parts as well as a full line of locks. All six floors of the factory had "outhouses" that hung out over the side of the building directly over the river.

After a fire destroyed the Eagle Lock factory, many of the buildings were razed in August of 1978. The remaining buildings were used until recently by Napco and are still used by the Allread Company, located on South Main Street.

Eagle Lock Corporation
ANNIVERSARY DINNER
For Retired Employees

Plymouth,

Connecticut

1795 - 1970

DODRASQUICENTENNIAL
ANNIVERSARY
May 9 — May 17
1970

In 1970, the town had its 175th anniversary. The word "Dodrasquicentennial" was researched by Mr. and Mrs. Vincent Klimas to describe this special anniversary. During the celebration, Eagle Lock Company retirees were honored, some for giving as much as sixty-five years of service to the company. Lingering problems and a strike finally forced the Eagle Lock Company to close in 1975.

Seven
Terryville Churches of the Past

The Immaculate Conception Church was built in 1882, but the parish did not get its own resident priest until 1900. The Fourth Degree Assembly of Knights of Columbus is named in honor of the Immaculate Conception's first priest, Reverend John Neale.

The Immaculate Conception Church is located next to Baldwin Park. A later renovation added a new front and simplified the church's original Victorian look.

The Saint Paul Evangelical Lutheran Church was organized in 1891 by German settlers and adopted its first constitution in January of 1892. The present church building was built in 1902 during the tenure of Pastor Otto Duessel of Bristol. Saint Paul received its own pastor, the Reverend H. Voight of the Iowa Synod, in 1905. Services were given both in German and English until 1932, when the Reverend A.M. Schroeder began services in English only.

In 1904, the Immaculate Conception Church erected the Lyceum building on Main Street for parish recreational and social activities. This is the site of the Terryville Furniture store.

The Saint Cyril and Methodius Russian Orthodox Church was started by twelve families in 1908, and the church was finally built on a lot at the corner of Ames and Fairview Avenues in 1912. A steeple and bell were added in 1920.

The interior of the Russian Orthodox Church is beautifully decorated in a characteristic Byzantine style. Donations of crosses and icons were added to the church interior in the early 1960s.

The Holy Trinity Evangelical Lutheran Church began as a part of the Saint Paul Evangelical Lutheran Church in 1892. Conflicts concerning the church's obtaining its own pastor divided the congregation, and by 1904, the Holy Trinity had become a separate congregation under the leadership of the Reverend Otto Duessel. The Holy Trinity congregation built its present church on Maple Street in 1911, after becoming affiliated with the Lutheran Church Missouri Synod in 1909.

Saint Michael's Ukrainian Catholic Church is located on Allen Street. It was built by Ukranian settlers from Pennsylvania who sought to preserve their Ukranian heritage and religion. Saint Michael's was built in 1910 but did not have its own resident priest until 1921.

Saint Casimir's Church was founded by the Polish community of Plymouth. Attracted by the industrial jobs of Eagle Lock and the Andrew Terry Foundry in the late nineteenth century, Polish settlers gravitated to the area and were anxious to preserve their Polish language and Catholic traditions. After conducting their Polish services in both the town hall and Lyceum Hall for many years, the congregation blessed the new Polish church on Allen Street in 1906.

Saint Casimir's Hall was a frequent host to fund-raisers, athletic events, receptions, community breakfasts, and church activities. Town meetings were regularly held here as well. Built in 1939 by the Saint Casimir's Society, the hall was indeed a popular place.

Trolley tracks pass the Congregational church and parsonage on Main Street. The charming and ornate parsonage was torn down when the new Congregational church was built.

This older postcard view looks west in front of the Terryville Congregational Church and parsonage. The Terryville Town Hall is located on the right.

Congregational Church, Terryville, Conn.

The Terryville Congregational Church was formed in 1838 when some members of the Plymouth Congregational Church decided to move closer to the industrial area in Terryville. Eli Terry was an original member of the church and manufactured its tower clock. The clock remained there until fire destroyed the church in 1967. Two years later, a new church was built on the site of the original church.

Saint Mark's Episcopal Church on North Main Street was the town's smallest church. It was organized in 1901 and closed its doors as an Episcopal church in 1969.

Eight
The Holt District

The District No. 12 Holt School once stood on North Harwinton Avenue between the Holt and Fenn Farms. In 1880, teams of oxen dragged stone blocks up for the school's foundation. Teacher Andrew Buell taught there in the 1880s for a salary of $106.13 for the winter school term. In 1950, the Holt Community Club was organized to keep the one-room school open; it was unable to convince taxpayers of the institution's importance and the Holt School was closed in 1957.

Still maintained as a private home belonging to Robert and Nancy Henderson, the Holt School is considered to be the last one-room schoolhouse in Connecticut. The Hendersons proudly display the old blackboard and a student desk in their home. People who once attended the school still appear on sunny days to take nostalgic photographs.

This early school bus for the Holt School seems to be a converted hay truck. Many people in the Town of Plymouth remember attending the Holt School.

Children of the Holt School all dressed in their best clothes pose for this picture taken in the early years of this century. Teacher Hattie Buell is seated in the back row on the right.

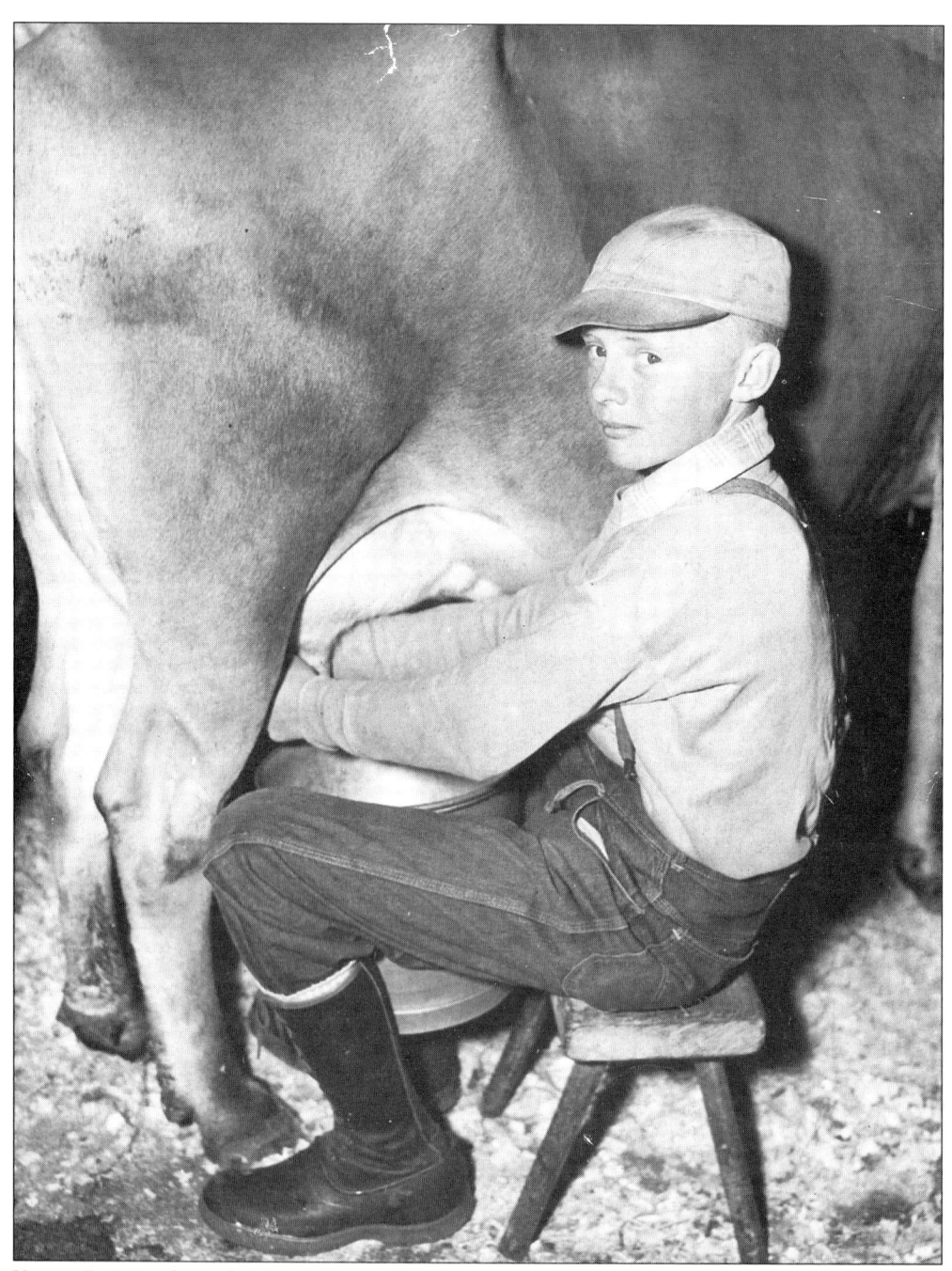

Young Raymond Armbruster, who is about thirteen years old in this picture, milks one of the family cows in the early 1940s. The farm sold the milk from the fifty to one hundred cows to the Freimuth, Elton, and Guida Milk Companies. Ray, who was born in the old farmhouse, was the youngest of ten children, two of whom were Heberle step-siblings.

The Armbruster Farm was once owned by the Holt family, for which the Holt District was named. The old farmhouse—shown here in an early picture—includes a woodshed sled in the foreground, which was used to bring in wood or potatoes from the fields. In 1919, Frank and Caroline Armbruster bought the farm for their sons Philip and Carl. Philip and his wife Caroline built it up into a 340-acre dairy farm, the last working farm in the Town of Plymouth.

The Minor Farm was originally purchased in 1855 by Hiram and Sarah Minor. Hiram's son Maurice ran a sawmill and a horse and dairy farm for many years. The Minor Homestead—shown here in a picture dated 1940—was originally the home of the farm help, but was later purchased by Maurice Minor from his father. Maurice's daughter Emily and her husband, Carl Miller, lived in the house until their deaths; Judy Cumiskey, their daughter, lives there now with her family.

Philip Armbruster, known as "Pa" to most of his family and neighbors, poses with a team of draft horses that helped to work the large dairy farm. Today Philip's son Raymond, and Raymond's son Todd, still grow hay and raise beef cattle and horses.

Maurice and Fannie Taylor Minor were married in October 1913. Here they pose, perhaps before a "dress-up Sunday drive," with their new son Kenneth in a fine horse and sulky.

Kenneth Minor cranks up the old model "sport utility vehicle" for his wife Margaret on the Minor Farm while a team of oxen look on at the newfangled machine.

Carl Miller, Elbert Minor, and Maurice Minor (on top) bring in the hay with a wagon pulled by the farm's oxen.

Carol Minor Orr stands by her prize-winning Devon ox team at the Terryville Fair in 1957. Not many girls showed oxen in those days, so her prize was a great honor.

Maurice Minor poses with the steam engine that he used to run his sawmill and horse farm. The steam engine is now housed in the Plymouth Historical Society's building on Main Street. Maurice Minor served five terms in the Connecticut Legislature, from 1917 to 1921 and from 1951 to 1957. He lived to be one hundred and a half years old.

The Minor family enjoys going fishing. Uncle Charles Minor looks approvingly at his nieces, Carol and Lorraine, and his nephew, Lawrence Minor, before heading out for a morning of fishing. The outing was complete with a can of worms, some fishing poles, and sun hats.

Ed Borkoski with his oxen and Ray Armbruster with a team of horses take Carl Miller's steam engine to the Plymouth Historical Society building the old-fashioned way.

Nine
People Who Serve

"AH! NEVER SHALL THE LAND FORGET
HOW GUSHED THE LIFE-BLOOD OF THE BRAVE!"

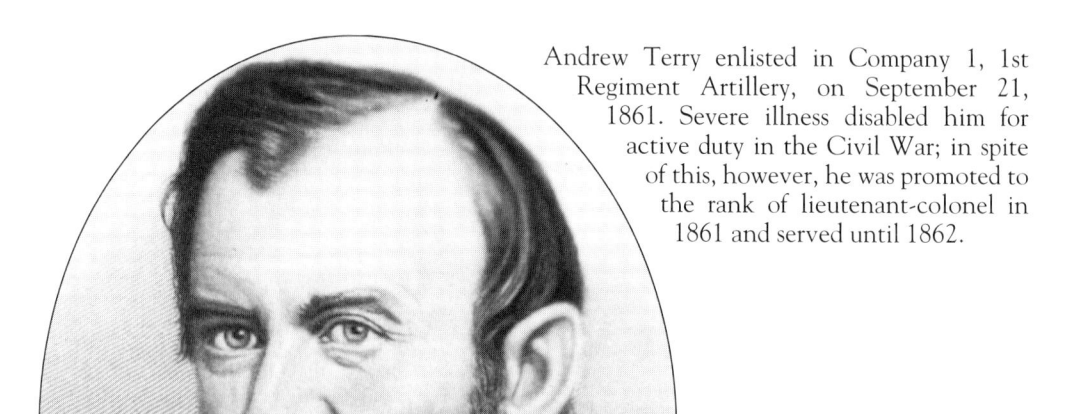

Andrew Terry enlisted in Company 1, 1st Regiment Artillery, on September 21, 1861. Severe illness disabled him for active duty in the Civil War; in spite of this, however, he was promoted to the rank of lieutenant-colonel in 1861 and served until 1862.

Eugene Atwater, another Civil War veteran, enlisted on October 23, 1861, as a private first class in the 1st Light Battery. He was promoted to captain in February 1865 and mustered out six months later.

A celebration on the Plymouth Green in the 1920s honored the last surviving Plymouth veterans of the Civil War. George Bates, on the extreme right of the picture, served with the 2nd Connecticut Volunteer Heavy Artillery and was wounded at Winchester, Virginia.

Donald Leach posed in his World War I uniform with his father, Marshall W. Leach, before heading for the war in Europe. He was killed in action in France on August 5, 1918, the first Plymouth man to be killed in the war.

The *Waterbury American* newspaper article the day after Donald Leach's death gave the details of Donald's service to his country and of the supreme sacrifice he made. Many years later, Mrs. Marshall Leach traveled as a Gold Star Mother to her son's grave in France.

PLYMOUTH BOY PAYS SUPREME SACRIFICE

Donald Leach, Killed in Action, Enlisted in H Company.

SENDOFF FOR DRAFTEES

Crowd Bids Latest Contingent Godspeed—Red Cross Report.

Thomaston, Aug 6.

Mr and Mrs Marshall Leach of Plymouth received a telegram yesterday afternoon from the War Department stating their son, Donald, had been killed in action in France. Donald enlisted in Company H, Second Regiment of Waterbury on May 5, 1917, which with the First Regiment afterwards merged into the 102d United States Infantry. This regiment it will be remembered had an accident at sea caused by the breaking of the propeller of the ship on which they were being transported to France and which necessitated their returning to an Atlantic port for repairs. Donald eLach was well and favorably known in town, although residing just outside the town limits, and Mr and Mrs Leach have many friends in this community. They naturally grieve over the loss of their son, but are consoled by the fact that he died bravely fighting in the defense of humanity and justice.

Assigned to the Missouri.

The Terryville Fire Station and firetruck were housed beside the Terryville Town Hall before they were moved to the North Main Street station across from the park.

This picture, dated 1928, shows the pride of the Terryville Fire Department—a White Buffalo firetruck.

A brand new firetruck is parked in Baldwin Park directly in front of the North Main Street fire station. A new firehouse was built on Harwinton Avenue in Terryville in 1971. On February 7, 1972, the old firehouse became the home of the Plymouth Volunteer Ambulance Corps, which had housed its vehicles for four years in various garages and buildings around town.

Fire Chief Cornelius Carrington poses in parade dress in 1925. Carrington was once a custodian at the Prospect Street School and he served with the volunteer fire department for many years.

In this 1961 photograph, fireman Matt Halpern shows off the first cup won by the Terryville Fire Department. When the TFD was in active competition, they won numerous awards, many of which are visible behind Matt.

A giant tree that was knocked over in a 1950s storm is being cleared off Route 6. Huge maples and elms once lined most of Route 6 through Terryville and Plymouth.

These Terryville beauties were a featured part of the 50th Anniversary Firemens' Parade in 1961. Pat Bunnell Packer received the crown, and Cathy Gleason Kosak (on the left) was first runner-up. The other finalists were Joanne Stucjus and Pam Klepps Hackling (in front) and Roseanne Gervais Witbeck (in back).

Original members of the Plymouth Volunteer Ambulance Corps were honored in 1984 and given PVAC Life Member Cards. Pictured here are Ed Lausier, Elmer Bates, and John Hamel. Ed Lausier still runs a barber shop on Main Street in Terryville and continues to canvas every year for the annual ambulance fund drive.

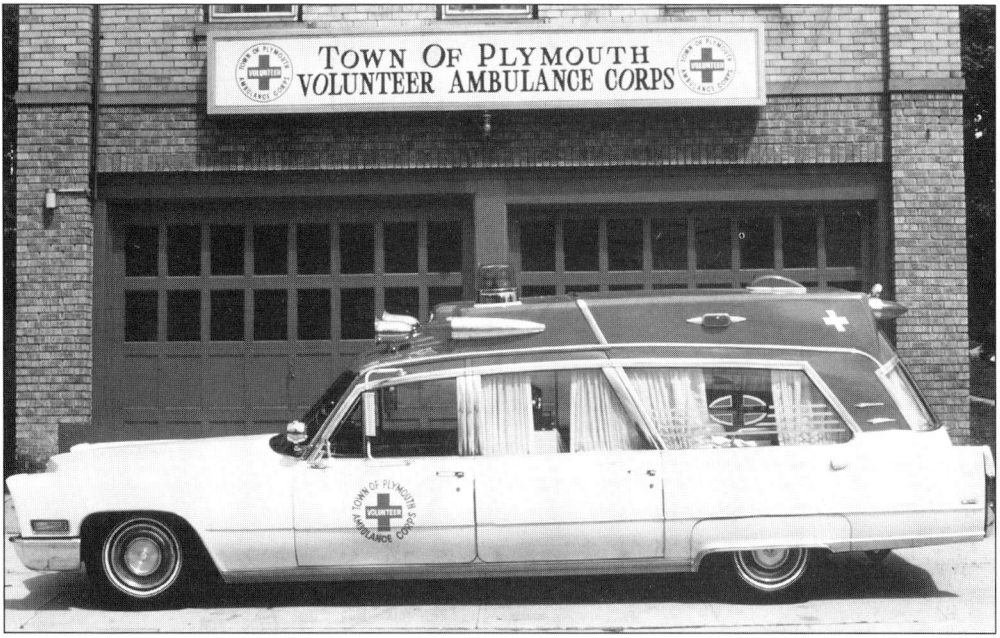

The first ambulance was a Cadillac donated by the Terryville Lions Club in 1968. Terryville Lion Truman Gustafson led the crusade for a volunteer ambulance corps and became the first chairman of the Plymouth Volunteer Ambulance Corps Board of Directors.

PVAC members put up the sign announcing the beginning of the annual door-to-door fund drive in Baldwin Park in front of corps headquarters.

Members of the PVAC pose before heading out to man the first aid and water stations located along the very long route of the 1995 bicentennial parade, which finished up at the Terryville Fairgrounds.